TWO
ROADS

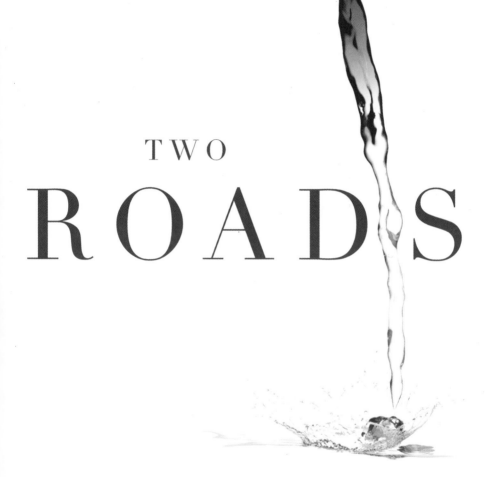

A 4-Part Group Study
of *The Cure*

THE TRUEFACE TEAM

Cover & Interior Design by Outskirts Studio

Produced by **Trueface**
Trueface.org
ISBN: 978-1-7348805-9-5

Printed in the United States.

Contents

NOTES

Getting Started

Welcome! We're excited for you to go on this journey. This guide is based on the first three chapters of *The Cure*, Trueface's flagship, foundational book. It's for people who have already read *The Cure* as well as those who are brand new to it, and the sections of *The Cure* that we'll be looking at are all included in this guide. This study is designed to help you cultivate your own community of grace right where you are.

Trueface studies are built with the same overall structure and flow within your meetings. The overall structure is:

Week 1: > **Week 2:** > **Week 3:** > **Week 4:**
RELATIONSHIP   STORY   STUDY   LIVE

We begin with an emphasis on the foundation of **relationships**, because grace is always experienced in the context of relationships. Then, we follow Jesus's example of using **stories** to help us understand how truth and grace come together. We then dig into scripture and **study** what God's Word says about the topic. Lastly, we go and **live**, because isn't that what following Christ is really about?

WITHIN EACH MEETING, WE GO THROUGH THE SAME THREE SECTIONS:

Connect

We spend time connecting with each other in order to grow in our relationships.

Learn

We use content to help us learn and as a catalyst for growth.

Live

We discuss and apply what we learned to our actual lives, so that we can live out and experience these truths. We ask ourselves questions like:

- What does this mean for me personally?
- What step is God inviting me to take?
- How can we help each other?

TRUEFACE

beyond the mask

Today's culture is perfecting the art and science of creating masks. Behind these masks, people are dying inside. **We're here to change that.**

Trueface equips people to **experience the freedom of living beyond the mask.** When we increase trust in our relationships, we are able to experience being more **authentically known and loved** by God and others.

We hope to be a bridge for hundreds of thousands to experience the peace and freedom of the original good news by trusting God and others with their whole selves.

To learn more about Trueface, visit *trueface.org*, or join the thousands of people living the Trueface life on social media.

🅾 **Instagram:** @truefacelife

🅵 **Facebook:** @truefacecommunity

🅣 **Twitter:** @truefaced

To become a Trueface Partner through monthly giving and join the group that allows us to continue creating resources like the one you're about to experience, visit *trueface.org/give*.

Logistics

You'll find the videos for this study at *trueface.org/two-roads-group.* The videos are free to use and are broken up by each meeting. Each week has five Digging Deeper sections for you to read or listen to if you'd like to process the study more fully. The audio for these sections is at *trueface.org/two-roads-group* as well.

Below is a place for you to write down what dates you'll be meeting, where you'll be meeting, and the most important thing—who'll be bringing the food!

MEETING 1: RELATIONSHIP

What road am I on?

Date: _____

Location: _____

Snacks: _____

MEETING 2: STORY

What mask am I wearing?

Date: _____

Location: _____

Snacks: _____

MEETING 3: STUDY

Who am I?

Date: _____

Location: _____

Snacks: _____

MEETING 4: LIVE

How could this change my life?

Date: _____

Location: _____

Snacks: _____

Week 1

What road am I on?

MEETING TOGETHER

Have someone read this out loud:

Welcome to Two Roads: The Cure Group Study! We're excited that this group is about to engage on this journey.

During this first time together, we will place a greater emphasis on connecting in our relationships. We will get to know each other a little more and get on the same page so that we can go on this journey together.

Every time we meet we'll have three sections to our time together: Connect, Learn, and Live. Let's get started!

Connect

THIS SECTION WILL TAKE ABOUT 40% OF YOUR TIME TOGETHER TODAY

As a group:

- Pray:

  » Have someone pray to open this study. Invite God to prepare your hearts to experience more of His love and for His Spirit to help guide the time together.

- Warm-up questions:

  » What is something you've done in the last sixty days that you've been proud of?

  » What are you looking forward to in this study?

Now take ten minutes to go through the questionnaire below individually. You don't need to share your answers—this is just for you.

WHERE AM I?

On a scale of 1-5, how much do you agree or disagree with the following statements?

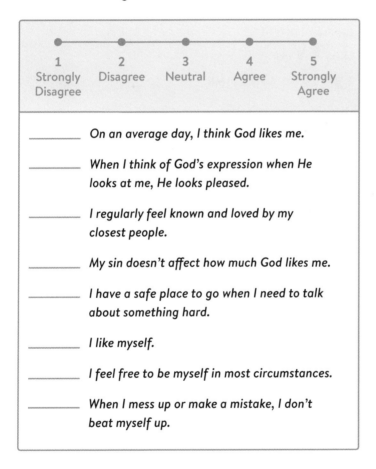

1	2	3	4	5
Strongly Disagree	Disagree	Neutral	Agree	Strongly Agree

_____ *On an average day, I think God likes me.*

_____ *When I think of God's expression when He looks at me, He looks pleased.*

_____ *I regularly feel known and loved by my closest people.*

_____ *My sin doesn't affect how much God likes me.*

_____ *I have a safe place to go when I need to talk about something hard.*

_____ *I like myself.*

_____ *I feel free to be myself in most circumstances.*

_____ *When I mess up or make a mistake, I don't beat myself up.*

While you are waiting for others to finish their questionnaire, think about how your answers reflect your view of God and yourself. Once everyone has finished this section, move on to the video.

NOTES

Learn

 10% OF YOUR TIME

> ▷ **WATCH THE RELATIONSHIP VIDEO.**
> You'll find this at *trueface.org/two-roads-group.*

Live

◑ **50% OF YOUR TIME**

DISCUSS:

We want to help you build a Room of Grace right here in this group. After you watch the video, choose a few questions from the list below to process together. Do your best to not give the answer you think you're supposed to—try to be as authentic and real as you can.

1. Which road do you think you've most often walked—the road of Pleasing God or the road of Trusting God? Where do you think you are today?

2. "God loves you always, but He likes you a lot less when you mess up."

   "God is delighted with you, wild about you, regardless of how you behave."

   Which of these two statements is closer to how you view God?

NOTES

10

③ The video talks about two rooms: one with people that seem put together but masked, and one with people that are messy but honest. Which is a closer description of your experiences with other Christians?

④ Who do you trust enough to show your true face? What makes you trust them?

⑤ For some of us, believing that God loves and likes us all the time sounds dangerous. Do you agree? Why or why not?

APPLY:

Move your group discussion into how we can grow in these areas by asking the following questions.

- What would it look like for you to start living more out of trusting God instead of pleasing God in your everyday life?

- What is one practical, tangible way you can create more of a Room of Grace in your life this week? Is there a step God is inviting you to take? Some ideas are below:

  » Call a friend to ask how they're doing and then share something real in return.

  » Share with one trusted person that you'd like for them to know more of the real you. This can help lay the foundation for future conversations.

NOTES

» Grab coffee with someone you trust and share about the concept of being put together but masked versus being messy but honest. Share the ways you think you've experienced both.

» Make a list of what you think are your go-to masks and try to take one off this week.

» Anything else come to mind? Be creative, but practical. Try to make it an actionable step in order to help integrate your actions with your beliefs.

• How I'm going to live it out (*yes, we're having you write it down to help you remember—it's a useful trick!*):

• How can the group come alongside you in this, even if it's a really small step? Letting other people actually love and walk with you is a foundational piece of building a Room of Grace.

- Look ahead to the *Digging Deeper* material for a deeper dive into these two roads. You can either read these five sections between now and your next meeting or listen to the audio of them by visiting *trueface.org/two-roads-group.* If you don't get to them, that's okay. You won't get as much processing time in this study, but don't let that keep you from your community.

- Pray to close out this time together.

NOTES

Digging Deeper

If you're a visual learner, over the next seven days (or however long you're taking between meeting together) read these five sections and reflect on the questions at the end. If you're an auditory learner or would prefer to listen on your commute or while you work on a project, we've provided the audio for each day at *trueface.org/two-roads-group.*

You can do them all at once, but we suggest breaking the five sections over multiple days to give yourself more processing time. This week's sections are from Chapter 1 of *The Cure*.

If you aren't able to go through the five sections before your next meeting, **that's okay.** Don't let it stop you from connecting with your community.

Section 1:

You can find the audio file of this section at trueface.org/two-roads-group.

NOTES

When you're young, the life ahead of you is a pristine, never opened book. It has that intoxicating new book smell. You've just cracked the cover, the pages are white and clean, and you absolutely know there's a grand story ahead. When you're very young, you could be a cowboy or a ballerina. In the glory of youth, you and your friends are dread pirates, widely adored pop stars, superstar athletes, gallant knights, or a queen whose rule is just and kind. Later, the fantasies fade, but the dreams become more focused. Maybe you'll be the first human being on Mars or the doctor who cures breast cancer. The story is whatever you want it to be, and you're still in the opening pages of your great novel. You know, though, that the story will be great. You know you have a destiny, a purpose in this life. Some of those dreams are your own, it's true. But some of those dreams, those hopes of destiny, are from God.

As we grow older, some of those dreams begin to fade, washed in pain, cynicism, and failure. The edges tatter, the thread grows bare, and sometimes the fabric falls away completely. Something unnamed repaints the horizon. The mundane, agonizing details of life build and build like bricks. Soon we are too weary of wrestling with our everyday existence to entertain grand visions of destiny. Even our relationship with God, which seemed so wonderfully beautiful and life-giving at first, dims.

We don't stop walking, but we may as well. What toxin is this that can turn a wide-eyed dream into a grinding drudge? It's as if we all woke up one morning under a curse we couldn't shake. We push on, one foot in front of the other, but we stop wondering why. The next thing we know, we've got rocks in our shoes and lungs lined with dust. The curse is not a metaphor, though. The curse is a lie all of us buy into, sometimes suddenly, sometimes slowly, like a frog in a pot. The lie breaks our hearts, and it scatters us in different ways. Some of us find shelter in religious discipline. Some seek solace in cynicism and unchecked deconstruction. Some are driven away completely.

Then we place blame: on ourselves, others close to us, our religious systems, the government, fluoridated water, or God Himself. Some of this blame is valid, for sure. Some of the places that should have been safest perpetuated the lie the loudest.

Here is the lie, in two parts:

We do not see God as He is,
and we do not see ourselves as we are.

I don't even notice at first. But suddenly the ten feet in front of me are going different ways. And, I realize I have no idea which way to go. I'm staring at the intersection like this could make it go away. That's when I notice the tall pole with two arrows at the top pointing down each fork. What's written on them is even more confusing than the fork. One arrow,

NOTES

pointing left, reads Pleasing God. The one leading right reads Trusting God. You're kidding. I'm supposed to choose between these two? I'm not doing that. Choosing one means not choosing the other. It's like being asked to choose between your heart and lungs. What I want is a bypass. But there is no bypass.

I look up at the Trusting God sign. This has to be a trap, a trick question. It sounds good, but it doesn't give me anything to do. It's too passive. How will I make a difference? If God and I are going to be in sync, there's got to be something more than trust. If the issue is me, I'm probably not going to figure out my destiny simply by trusting that God can be trusted!

I move over to the Pleasing God sign pointing down the path to the left. This has to be it! After all He's done for me, the very least I can do is please Him.

So, I set off on the path of pleasing God, shaded by towering oaks. I'm encouraged to see this path is well-traveled, beaten level with the feet of a million travelers. Many of them, in fact, are still on the path. The first group I pass is a trio of buskers, strumming guitars and a mandolin. We nod to each other politely. A little while on, there's a family of five camping just thirty yards off the path, next to a brook. Even farther, a middle-aged couple basks in the sun by the side of the road.

"Hello!" I wave. "Will I see you later on?"

"Nope." The man is smiling, but firm. "We left the Room of Good Intentions some time ago. We can't see going back."

"Okay," I respond, confused. I'm not sure what the "Room of Good Intentions" is, but not everyone wants to please God, I guess. After a long while, passing many more travelers by the wayside, I see a giant building looming in the distance. It looks like a hotel. As I get closer, I can see there's writing in bronze lettering across the front:

Striving Hard to Be All God Wants Me to Be.

Finally. Something for me to do. I strive after success in my career. I strive after keeping fit. Why would it be any less with God?

I draw closer and notice a door. Above the doorknob, a small, ornate plaque is bolted to the heavy wooden door. Self-Effort it reads. Of course! God does His part, and I do mine. It's about time someone said it.

I turn the handle and walk in.

I'm stunned to find a huge open room filled with thousands of people. I scan the group, trying to take it all in. "So, these are the people really living for Jesus." Soon I notice there's a woman, a hostess maybe, standing next to me. She is immaculately groomed. Every hair is perfectly in place, her makeup accentuating her features, her smile is wide and toothy. Nothing about her seems out of place.

"Welcome to the Room of Good Intentions."

She says it clean and cool, like she's been greeting people all her life. There's just the tiniest little shred about it that's unsettling, but I'm so excited to finally be here I don't think much of it.

"You have no idea how long I've waited to find this place!" I return her smile, grasping her primly outstretched hand. I call out to the crowd, almost involuntarily, "Hey, how's everyone doing?"

The room goes silent. It's full of beautiful people, smiling people. Some of them wear elaborately crafted masks, which is great because I love masquerades. This looks like my kind of place. One man steps forward. His smile, like the hostess, is broad. His bleached white teeth look as if they had been lined up by a ruler.

"Welcome," he begins, shaking my hand firmly. "We're fine. Thank you for asking. Just fine. Aren't we, everyone?" A few in the crowd behind him nod, smiling along. "My kids are doing great and . . . um . . . I'm about to close some very lucrative deals at work. More fit than when I was in high school, I'm telling you. I'm doing just fine. Everyone here is."

Before I can reflect on how strange that sounded, the hostess asks how I'm doing. "Me? Well, to be honest,

I've been struggling with some stuff. That's partly why I'm here. I'm trying to figure out . . ."

"Shhhhh," she interrupts me, putting a flawlessly manicured index finger to her lips. She reaches behind a podium and pulls out a mask, handing it to me. She nods her head with a curt smile, indicating I should put it on. I stare at it for a moment. Others in the room are excitedly motioning for me to do so. Slowly, I slide the mask over my face.

My next thought is it might be best to back off on the self-revelation. I find myself answering, as if from somewhere far away, "You know, I'm great. I'm doing fine!" And everyone in the room smiles before returning to their conversations.

SCRIPTURE

Jeremiah 29:11

REFLECT:

What did you dream about becoming when you were younger? How has that changed over the years?

Where have you experienced the idea that you should be striving hard to be all God wants you to be in your own life?

Think of a time someone encouraged you to put on a mask, like the hostess did, even if they didn't do it intentionally. How did that affect you?

Section 2:

You can find the audio file of this section at trueface.org/two-roads-group.

This is the Room of Good Intentions.

The main entrance hall is massive and ornate. Winding stairways lead to upper levels, where cascading fountains are ringed with beautifully upholstered sofas and chairs. There are doorways leading to ballrooms, dining halls, and fancily appointed living quarters. Everything is white marble and gold leaf. It's gorgeous and opulent. Across the back wall there's a huge, embroidered banner.

WORKING ON MY SIN TO ACHIEVE AN INTIMATE RELATIONSHIP WITH GOD, IT READS.

Finally, someone's saying what I've experienced all these years. Early on, when I first believed, He and I were so close. Then over time I kept failing. I'd do something stupid. I'd promise I wouldn't do it anymore. Then I'd fail at the same thing again. Before long, it felt like He was on the other side of an ever-growing pile of the garbage I'd created. I imagined Him farther away each day, with His arms folded, shaking His head, thinking, I had so much hope for this kid, but he's let me down so many times.

But looking across this room, I know now I can change all that. This room—it's impressive. The decorations are nice enough, but you can feel the

NOTES

NOTES

courage and diligence. You can almost taste the full-hearted fervency, the accomplishment, the head-on determination.

There's the Fortune 500 executive who has given away ninety percent of his wealth to charity. There is the lead pastor of a thriving network of churches, a dynamic communicator whose theological insights are heard the world over. I meet a girl, elegant even in her simple, worn clothes, who has devoted nearly all her energy to providing medical supplies to the Untouchables in Kolkata.

So many good-hearted people fill this room. They have devoted themselves to God, to studying His character, to pouring themselves into spreading His Word, to serving humanity in the name of Jesus. This must be it! Soon God and I will be close again.

Weeks run into months in this room, and a slight unease starts to creep in. It gets stronger by the day, but I can't put my finger on it at first. I'm noticing many in here talk in a sort of semi-joking, put-down banter. It's familiar, but a bit off. And standing this long on the edges of insider conversations, I realize I never noticed how annoying or obvious the subtle bragging sounds.

Even through those elaborate masks, I'm struck with how tired everyone looks. Many conversations are superficial and guarded. Several times, I've caught the real faces of people with masks removed when they thought no one was looking. There is a deep, lonely pain in their expressions.

I'm starting to think differently, too. The comfort I felt when I got here is fading. I'm carrying this tension, like if I don't measure up, I'll be shunned. Oh, and with God too! Here's another thing: despite all my passionate sincerity, I keep sinning. Then I get fixated on trying not to sin. Then it all repeats: same sin, same thoughts, same failure.

I spend more time alone now. It's hard to be in public very long before my mask starts to itch fiercely. I spend more time preparing to be with people than I spend actually being with people. I can't seem to do enough to make these people, or God for that matter, happy.

Increasingly, the path to pleasing God seems to be about how I can keep God pleased with me.

One day it dawns on me what I've been doing to myself and to everyone around me. I've been trying to meet some lofty expectation, primarily to gain acceptance from people. I don't even know why I'm performing for them. To satisfy a God I'm not sure I can ever please? Even worse, I expect everyone around me to do the same.

• • •

There's no denying the appeal of the Room of Good Intentions. But the room is predicated on a lie, producing many sad consequences.

NOTES

For instance, when we embrace the path to this room, we reduce godliness to a formula:

More right behavior + Less wrong behavior = Godliness

There's only one thing wrong with the equation: it completely disregards the righteousness God has already placed in us. Yes, we mature in godliness, but if we disregard the righteousness that results from trusting what God has done in us, we're hiding who we truly are.

This path is cruel in its heroic-sounding deception, partly because it never allows us to see a fundamental truth:

We can never resolve our sin by working on it.

We may externally sublimate behavior, but we're essentially repositioning the chairs a bit on the deck of a sinking ship. When we strive to sin less, we don't. Worse, the whole hamster wheel effort of it all causes us to lose hope that anything will ever break through. In fact, this path actually seals us in immaturity. Even though this distorted theology breaks our hearts over and over and over, we desperately keep trying it.

What a wicked hoax.

SCRIPTURE:

Galatians 3:5-6

REFLECT:

When you think of things you need to "take care of" in order to be closer to God, what comes to mind?

In the Room of Good Intentions, we feel like we receive God's favor depending on how well we're performing. How do you experience this in your life?

"We can never resolve our sin by working on it." Why might the enemy want to keep us focused on trying to fix our sin?

You can find
the audio file of
this section at
trueface.org/two-
roads-group.

NOTES

Section 3:

Now I'm frantically working my way through the room, searching for someone—anyone—willing to talk about what's going on inside me. But nobody wants to hear it. It's as if they fear expressing my concerns will expose theirs.

So, even though I was certain this room might be my only real chance of getting it right, I find myself slipping out the door unnoticed. I thought I'd never leave, and I'm crushed.

A few hours later I'm sitting down at the grassy edge of the path, back at the fork in the road. That middle-aged couple is there, too, lounging on the other side of the path in the shade of a tree. The man smiles, with a hint of disillusionment; it's one of the more natural smiles I've seen in a while.

"That place is weird, huh? I'm glad we got out of that mess," he says, spitting out his words with a twisting smile.

I nod my assent, and he takes a deep breath before leaning back to join his napping wife.

Now what?

My eyes drift back up to that sign, and I read the arrow pointing down the road to the right. Trusting God.

I shake my head, look up, and ask the sky, "Is there a third road?" Nothing. Even the couple across the path is snoring. I sigh as I climb to my feet, brush myself off, and head down the right fork.

The path is rougher here, rutted and pockmarked with stones. It's a little steeper and slower going, but prettier, too. There are roughly hewn stone bridges over fast-flowing creeks and scenic vistas over vast, green valleys. After several hours, I see another huge building in the distance. When I finally reach it, I see these words emblazoned in tall bronze letters across the facade:

Living Out of Who God Says I Am.

That's supposed to help me how? I've been trying to live out what God wants me to be this whole time.

Again, there's a huge wooden double door, and again there's a plaque over the knob. But this time there's only one word written over it.

Humility.

Suddenly every effort of this entire journey collapses on me. Tears I've kept back so long well up as I mumble through my sobs, "I'm so tired. I can't do it. Help me. God, You're wiser, more right, and more loving. And I have not let You love me. I've fought so hard to impress You, and none of it did. Now I'm weary, empty, and alone. I'm tired of performing. I'm tired of pretending I can please You by any amount of effort. Help me, my God!"

After minutes in front of that door, I wipe my wet eyes and nose on my sleeve. I run my fingers through my hair and desperately pull myself together. If this is anything like last time, I want to make a good first impression, and puffy eyes and tear-streaked cheeks won't do. Finally, I reach for the knob.

Inside, it's much like the other room. The layout is nearly the same, though the décor is toned down. The gold leaf and marble are replaced by warm carved wood and polished stone. The intricate details in every adornment are conspicuously missing, replaced by tasteful simplicity. Instead of sofas draped in shimmering silk, there are overstuffed couches and chairs. There are also more windows. Natural light pours in and I can see the views outside are breathtaking. Glass doors lead out onto porches and decks scattered with Adirondack chairs. Another hostess approaches. Like the hostess in the Room of Good Intentions, she is gorgeous, but her beauty is natural. She smiles, and I notice her eyes are smiling too. I realize with a start that the other hostess never smiled with her eyes. In a voice as beautiful as anything I've ever heard, she says, barely above a whisper, "Hello. Welcome to the Room of Grace."

Then, with a pause and a smile, she clasps my hands in hers, "How are you?"

The last time I answered this one, I was handed a mask. This hostess is nicer, but I'm not convinced.

"Fine. I'm doing fine . . ."

The whole room is watching me now, and I see eyebrows tilted in skepticism. My heart sinks. I'm so tired of this. I turn toward the room, all eyes on me, and yell out so everyone can hear.

"Hey, everybody, listen up! I am not fine. Not fine at all! I haven't been fine for a long time. I'm tired, confused, angry, and afraid. I feel guilty and lonely, and that makes me even angrier! I'm sad most of the time and I pretend I'm not. My life is not working at the moment! I'm so far behind and freaked out about what to do next, I'm almost completely frozen. And if any of you religious kooks knew half my daily thoughts, you'd kick me out of your little club. So, again, I'm doing not fine. Thanks for asking. I think I'll go now."

I turn toward the door before I have a chance to break down again. As I grab for the knob, a voice booms from the back of the room. "That's it? That's all you got? I'll take your anger, guilt, and dark thoughts and raise you compulsive sin and chronic lower-back pain! Oh, and did I mention I'm in debt up to my ears? I also wouldn't know classical music from a show tune if it jumped up and bit me! You'd better get more than that little list."

The room erupts in warm, genuine laughter, and I know it's not meant to embarrass me. The hostess leans in, nudges me, and kindly smiles. "I think he means you're welcome here."

I step into a crowd of welcoming smiles. And there's not a mask to be seen anywhere. Right away, I wish I'd known these people all my life.

You're in the Room of Grace! Grace! That word appears 122 times in the New Testament. The Judaizers in the apostle Paul's day hated it. They feared what it would do if it got loose. "Paul, you can't tell them this!" they said. "These people are immature, lazy, and have little religious background. They'll abuse it as soon as they can. They'll live Christianity-lite. These people are weak and want to do whatever they want. And believe me, what they want is not good." Paul responds, in essence, this way: "You'd have a great point, if it wasn't for two truths. First, these people have a new nature. They have Christ in them. They're not who they were. They don't want to get away with anything. They want to enjoy Him, and can't find a way to do that within your ugly system.

"Second, they have the Holy Spirit, who is able to correct, encourage, rebuke, and challenge. They have God, you know."

If you're looking for compliance, you can get that without God. Just wield enough power and people will do what you want them to. At least as long as you're around. But when you're out of sight, eventually—

inevitably—they'll revert to what they've been denied. The real trick is to allow the desires of the new heart to come out and have a run of the joint. We're hardwired for heartfelt obedience. We have to be religiously badgered into compliance, which leads to eventual disobedience. Only bad theology can do that. Sin and failure are all we think we have until new life is wooed forth. We need others to show us God beautifully, without condemnation, disgust, and unsatisfied demands. We long to obey Him. It makes our souls sing. We've just been goaded so long, we've learned to shield ourselves from religion. We'll fight that kind of authority just for the fight. It's what the Law does in any form. It makes rebels of people who want to love and be loved.

There's an incredible phrase in Hebrews: "Without faith it is impossible to please God." This statement shows us the path we must take. Only by trusting can we truly please God! If our primary motive is pleasing God, we'll never please Him enough and we'll never learn trust. Pleasing God is a good desire. It just can't be our primary motivation, or it'll imprison our hearts. If all we bring to God is our moral striving, we're back at the same lie that put us in need of salvation. We're stuck with our independent talents, longing, and resolve to make it happen. This self-sufficient effort to assuage a distant deity—it nauseates God.

When our primary motive becomes trusting God, however, we suddenly discover there is nothing in the world that pleases Him more!

Until you trust God, nothing you do will please God.

At that point, pleasing God is actually a by-product of trusting God. Pleasing is not a means to our godliness. It's the fruit of our godliness, for it's the fruit of trust. Trusting is the foundation of pleasing God. Lacking that basis of trust is like trying to build a house without a foundation.

The citizens of the Room of Grace get the privilege of experiencing the pleasure of God, because they have pleased God by choosing to trust Him. God has specific areas of our lives that He would like us to trust Him in, and looking for these opportunities is one of the best parts of the journey.

NOTES

SCRIPTURE:

1 Peter 5:6

REFLECT:

Why is humility necessary to enter a Room of Grace?

What areas of your faith life feel exhausting (yes, even if you know they're not "supposed to")? Which feel life-giving?

What is one area you feel like God is inviting you to trust Him in, instead of trying to please Him?

🎧

You can find the audio file of this section at **trueface.org/two-roads-group.**

NOTES

Section 4:

Eventually, I notice a banner in this room, too:

STANDING WITH GOD, MY SIN IN FRONT OF US, WORKING ON IT TOGETHER. I'M NOT SURE I GET IT YET.

· · ·

What if we could believe this is how God sees it, how it really is?

What if Christ, for the believer, is never over there, on the other side of our sin?

What if the power of His death on the cross allows Him to stand right in front of me on my worst day and smile bigger and happier than any human being ever could?

· · ·

That night, my loud new friend shows me to my room. It is simple and comfortable. The warm glow of a reading lamp bathes the room in a welcoming light. I'm happily exhausted from a seemingly endless parade of introductions during the day.

"Sleep well," my friend says, patting my shoulder firmly. "We're so glad you're here."

I take off my shoes and rub my sore feet, overwhelmed by it all. I'm tired, but the good kind of tired, like when you know you've put in a full day's work. I think back on the banner I read, and suddenly I know what it means. Before, God was always "over there," on the other side of my sin, obscured by the mound of trash between us. But now I realize He's here with me. I can picture it as clearly as if it's happening.

He puts His hands on my shoulders, staring into my eyes. No disappointment. No condemnation. Only delight. Only love. He pulls me into a bear hug so tight it knocks the breath out of me for a moment. At first, I feel unworthy. I want to push away and cry out, "I don't deserve this. Please stop. I'm not who you think I am!" But He does know. And soon I give in to His embrace. I hear Him say, "I know. I know. I've known from before time began. I've seen it all. I'm right here. I've got you."

And now I'm holding on with all my might. He stays right there in the moment until He's certain His love has been completely communicated and received. Only then does He release His grip so He can turn to put an arm around my shoulder. He then directs my sight to that mound of filth now out in front of us.

After several moments, He says with a straight face, "That is a lot of sin. A whole lot of sin. Don't you ever sleep?" He starts laughing. I start laughing.

NOTES

NOTES

Gazing at that mound of pain, I consider that I never thought I'd experience this kind of moment. All of the pain, regret, and damage of my life are laid out in front of me. All that have caused shame and condemnation. All that have caused me to pretend and impress and yearn for control. All that have broken my heart and His. But now I'm viewing it with Jesus's arm around me! He's been holding me with utter delight, all with my sin right here in our midst, never allowing it between us. He wants to know me in the midst of this, not when I get it cleaned up. I know now that if this mound is to ever shrink, it'll be by trusting this moment for the rest of my life.

He looks back at me. "We'll deal with this when you're ready. I've got your back."

I search His eyes, barely able to comprehend this love. Then it's over, and I'm back in my room. I'm asleep the moment my head hits the pillow.

The next morning, over fluffy waffles and bacon thick as a pork chop, I tell my new pajama-clad friend about the realization, how real it felt. He nods, grinning wildly.

"Yep, it's something, huh? We all experience something similar when we get here." He stabs a slice of pineapple with his fork. He winks knowingly. "You've got a lot more in store."

SCRIPTURE:

Romans 8:1

REFLECT:

Take a moment to imagine God with His arm around you, looking at your pain, failure, and sin. What are your top three emotions?

Think of one area of your life where you have sinned or failed or messed up somehow. How do you approach that area when you imagine God on the other side of your sin? What's your role or responsibility?

NOTES

How do you approach that area when you imagine God beside you with His arm around you? What's your role or responsibility?

You can find the audio file of this section at trueface.org/two-roads-group.

Section 5:

Wouldn't it be great if we could always stay right here? Some do.

They never again leave the Room of Grace and all its stunning, panoramic, life-giving surroundings, except to intentionally rescue and stand with those still outside.

However, many choose not to stay. As absurd as it sounds, some never even give themselves a chance to choose, a chance to get there. You see, not all make it back to the fork in the road after leaving the Room of Good Intentions. We call this the Wayside. Scattered along the entire path back towards the fork, you'll find them. Some sit alone, tucked away, almost out of sight. Some collect in twos and threes. Many spend the rest of their journey there. The Room of Good Intentions broke and jaded their hearts, robbing them of hope. It made them so sick that they're nearly anesthetized to believing life can ever be different. Man-made religion has beaten them down. Many are oozing with apathy. They can think of no good reason to try; they simply don't care. Some of God's most passionate, gifted, and dedicated servants are despondent along that road.

These wounded express themselves in many forms. Some are cynical and smug, but it's a cover. They're self-protecting from vulnerability. They're still

articulate and insightful—they just now speak from
the fringes of the arena. They're bleeding from having
risked vulnerability in a community that didn't know
what to do with it. Some are bitter, lashing out at
anything with more structure than an agreed upon
meeting time. Some create straw men, globalizing
their enemies into generalized categories so they can
ridicule them more easily.

When they do get together, they spend much of
the time rehearsing their wounds. They talk about
what they don't like. Their mantra is mistrust of any
authority. They brag of being free from the bondage
of religion, and they say this often in the same breath
they rehearse their wounded identity. They can no
longer remember the innocence of trust. They've
seen too much.

For a season, what they are doing can be right
and deeply corrective. They see from the vantage
point of having little left to lose. But after a while,
it makes them unforgiving, and there are now very
few surrounding them who can help guide them to
forgiveness.

No one matures in bitterness. No one gets free in
isolation. No one heals rehashing the testimonies of
bad religion. No one gets to love or be loved well in
self-protection.

Self-protection is one of the great oxymorons.
We're the only person in the world we don't have the
potential to protect. And once we hide from trusting

NOTES

God and others, we become more enflamed, more self-justified, more calloused in repeating our blame.

The ones along the road are accurate about their pain. Their wounds are real. So real, in fact, that they can't make it back by themselves to the fork in the road. They don't need an improved version of what they left. They smell manipulation in such an offer. Their senses have been heightened by pain. They too need the cure. Few destinies are more beautiful than the ones given to those who set out from the Room of Grace to find them.

The second reality is even harder to understand than the first.

NOTES

Not all stay in the Room of Grace once they've been there.

The Room of Grace is tricky business for those who've believed self-made excellence makes the person. For not only must we believe we are accepted, we must also learn to accept the yokels already here and the rookies who come in fresh each week! Oh, generous executives, successful pastors, and social justice workers are here too. But there is a vast difference. These made a life-altering choice back at the fork in the road. They're trusting who God says they are instead of adding up their behaviors to prove their godliness. They're convinced they can never resolve their sin by working on it. They know their sin is never between God and them. They live in the truth that there are no "together people."

They live careful and carefree because they realize the Father is crazy about them on their worst day.

They too must learn to rest in the sufficiency of Christ in them. If they stop trusting these stunning truths, they'll soon return to the familiar, the Room of Good Intentions.

For those of us weary of pretending, weary of being weary, we've found our home in the Room of Grace. It's where God and I live together, along with all who dare to trust that God sees us this way.

Whenever you're tempted to think you don't belong, that you've failed too often, failed too big, or are not meant to be close to God—just then, someone, maybe sitting very close to you, will smile and kindly say, "That's all you got?!" It's their way of saying, "You're welcome here."

SCRIPTURE:

Hebrews 11:6

NOTES

REFLECT:

How would you describe the Wayside? How have you experienced this in your life?

"They're bleeding from having risked vulnerability in a community that didn't know what to do with it." When have you had this experience, either as the one risking vulnerability or the one that doesn't know what to do with someone else's vulnerability?

Why is the Room of Grace hard for people that have done well in the Room of Good Intentions?

Week 2

What mask am I wearing?

MEETING TOGETHER

This week, we're going to experience someone's story of living in the Room of Good Intentions and the Room of Grace. Stories are helpful. Jesus taught us in stories because He knew that they would help us access truth in a different way than a list of instructions.

Connect

30% OF YOUR TIME

NOTES

As a group:

- Pray to open this time together. Who wants to volunteer?

- Warm-up question:

  » What is the number one thing you're looking forward to in the next month?

- Check in questions:

  » Last week we talked about practical, tangible ways we can build Rooms of Grace in our lives. How did that play out this week?

  » How did our last time together make you feel about this group?

  » What stood out to you this week, either from our conversation last time or the Digging Deeper material? What questions came up?

Learn

 20% OF YOUR TIME

> **WATCH THE STORY VIDEO.**
> You'll find this at *trueface.org/two-roads-group.*

Live

50% OF YOUR TIME

DISCUSS:

Choose a few questions that jump out to you from the list below to process as a group. Do your best to not give the answer you think you're supposed to—try to be as authentic and real as you can.

1. What stood out to you about T. A. (the pastor) and Betty (his wife)'s story?

2. What might have been different if T. A. and Betty hadn't felt like they needed to hide?

3. When have you felt like you needed to be the "together person" in your life?

4. Are you willing to share a few of the main masks you wear with the group?

NOTES

5 Which do you primarily identify yourself as: a sinner or a saint who still sins? How does it feel to think of yourself as a sinner? How does it feel to think about yourself as a saint who still sins?

6 How do you feel about T. A.'s statement that, "There's not going to be a time in our life where we don't sin anymore. But we're saints who sin. God gives me the gift of repentance. And that's grace?"

APPLY:

Move your group discussion into how we can grow in these areas by asking the following questions.

- What would it look like for you to live less masked in your everyday life?

- In this coming week's Digging Deeper material, we're going to look more closely at our masks and what drives us to wear them. What is one practical, tangible way that you can live beyond the mask this week? Ideas to get you started:

  » Check in with a friend right before a situation where you often put a mask on (e.g. an important meeting, a phone call with your mom, a particular friend group, etc.).

  » Give someone you trust permission to tell you when they think you're being masked this week. This might be someone in the group or someone else you trust, but it should probably be someone that interacts with you often.

NOTES

» Set aside time every morning before you start the day with a prayer asking God to help you take your mask off. Think about the mask you most often wear, then remind yourself, "That's not who I really am. I don't have to pretend to be that person."

» Anything else come to mind? Be creative, but practical. Try to make it an actionable step in order to help integrate your actions with your beliefs.

• How I'm going to live it out:

• How can the group, or one member in the group, come alongside you in this?

• Pray to close out this time together.

NOTES

Digging Deeper

If you're a visual learner, over the next seven days (or however long you're taking between meeting together) read these five sections and reflect on the questions at the end. If you're an auditory learner and would prefer to listen to the sections, we've provided the audio for each day at *trueface.org/two-roads-group.*

You can do them all at once, but we suggest breaking the five sections over multiple days to give you more processing time. This week's sections are from Chapter 2 of *The Cure.*

If you aren't able to go through the five sections before your next meeting, that's okay. Don't let it stop you from connecting with your community.

53

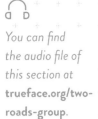

You can find the audio file of this section at **trueface.org/two-roads-group.**

NOTES

Section 1:

The day the hostess in the Room of Good Intentions handed me that mask, slipping it on felt very familiar. It felt safe. I'd been wearing one for a long, long time. I just wasn't aware of it.

Now, today, for the first time since before I can remember, I really believe I'm not wearing one. Just because I'm in the Room of Grace doesn't mean I won't put another back on, or so I'm told. But for today, at least, I think I'm me. Early this morning I walked out on the balcony deck off the first floor of the main hall. I sat down in an Adirondack chair, watching the sky as the sun rose and melted off the mist. My face felt cool in the early morning air. I forgot how much I miss feeling God's presence. This will take some getting used to. But everything is alive, less rehearsed, a little vulnerable, incredibly hopeful.

Here's my question: if this life of Christ in us is true—if there is no condemnation, if He's perfectly working to mature us from the inside out, and if He's absolutely crazy about us despite all our stuff— why would any of us ever put on a mask again?

. . .

I will—each of us will—be tempted to return to my mask each time I lose the confidence of my new identity.

Daring to trust who Christ says I am, who He says He is in me, even when I feel I least deserve it and the old shame sweeps over me—this is the only way to keep the mask off, to keep feeling the cool breeze on my face.

There are times when it seems like those of us who believe in Jesus are wearing more masks, and we seem to wear them more often than those who don't believe! What's with that? The truth is, we face even more pressure as followers of Jesus. We're tempted to don our masks even more if we haven't trusted our identity.

All of us are tempted to wear a mask when:

- We want to prove to others that we're worthy of their love.

- We want to prove to ourselves that we're worthy of being loved.

- We want others not to feel sorry for us.

- We fear if others see us truly, they won't want to know us.

- We want to be seen as great.

Believers in Christ additionally are tempted to wear a mask when:

- Our failures tell us the experiment of grace didn't work.

NOTES

- We want to prove to God that we're worth His choice to love us.

- We believe God wants us to fake it so He looks good.

- We want God to make our life work and our behavior seems like the price tag.

- We think God cares more about right behaviors than our trust and dependence.

- We think we're in competition with others, graded on a spiritual curve.

- Our shame makes us believe we must assuage God's disgust in us.

NOTES

SCRIPTURE:

Galatians 3:1-5

REFLECT:

We run back to our masks when we start to doubt our identity in Christ. What is one part of your identity in Christ that you most often doubt? Examples might be: that you are loved, worthy, righteous, enjoyed, accepted, etc.

Which of the temptations to wear a mask did you most resonate with?

If someone else told you that they wear that mask and why they wear it, what would you tell them? Do you believe what you would say?

You can find
the audio file of
this section at
trueface.org/two-
roads-group.

NOTES

Section 2:

Can you remember the first time you felt free enough
to talk to God honestly? When you discovered you
weren't hiding anything or pretending, no longer
talking to Him in manufactured religious jargon?
Maybe you'd just met Jesus, or maybe you first saw
Him for who He truly is, in all His majesty, glory,
and goodness. It's a moment of freedom, and raw,
unguarded hope like you'd never before imagined. It's
like you could feel your own blood pulsing through
your veins, so brightly alive! God waited an eternity for
this moment. He knew He couldn't fully reveal Himself
until He could cause you to risk trusting Him with who
you really were. It was stunning. It took fear away. It
broke lifelong patterns of dishonesty. People couldn't
figure out what happened to you. You were wildly
free, but safe. You were unguardedly alive, but more
caring. You were full of life-giving joy, but more deeply
sensitive to the pain in others. It painted your world in
colors you didn't even know existed. I had this same
experience. But something happened in the following
months and years. I lost confidence that His delight
and new life in me were strong enough to haul away
that giant mound of rotted cat food and mayonnaise,
the failures I presumed stood between Him and me. I
could point to aspects of my life that weren't changing
fast enough. So, I gradually bought the sales pitch
telling me I'd have to find something else, something
miraculous and mystical I'd receive if I could only
prove I cared enough. I set about gallantly propping
up my world.

Only now, because it was about God, the stakes were higher. I represented something other than just me, and the pressure was greater. Much greater. Soon, I was back to trying to impress a God I imagined was growing more and more impatient with me. I learned to bluff, manipulating and managing my persona to appear better than who I feared I was.

No one told me this two-faced life would severely stunt my growth. Or that it would break my heart. No matter how many titles and accolades I accumulate, I remain wounded and immature—long on "success," but short on dreams and substance. I admire people who live the Trueface life, but my loss of hope forces me to scramble for safety from behind a mask. The cost is horrific.

No one told me that when I wear a mask, only my mask receives love.

We can gain admiration and respect from behind a mask. We can even intimidate. But as long as we're behind a mask, any mask, we will not be able to receive love. Then, in our desperation to be loved, we'll rush to fashion more masks, hoping the next will give us what we're longing for: to be known, accepted, trusted, and loved.

This is no new phenomenon. Remember its source? God came in the cool of the day to be with Adam and Eve. He called out to a hiding Adam, "Where are you?" though He knew very well where Adam was. Adam

NOTES

59

responded, "I heard the sound of You in the garden, and I was afraid because I was naked; so I hid myself."

Afraid. Naked. Hidden. These were the first steps of a dance we've been stumbling to ever since. We become afraid because something we did or was done to us makes us feel naked. This nakedness cannot endure remaining uncovered. Nothing is more embarrassing or vulnerable than nakedness. Not knowing another option, we hide ourselves. Our dance now follows nearly identical steps. This shame—this self-awareness of their "uncleanness"—prompted Adam and Eve to fashion masks from leaves to hide what they now feared was true about them. It wasn't just that they'd done something wrong. They were both convinced something was now uniquely and terribly wrong about them, with them. This is how shame works, and it's different from guilt. Guilt wants to lead us to forgiveness, to be cleansed. Shame drives us to hide, convinced we cannot truly be forgiven or made clean. It forced them and has forced us to cover ourselves with whatever is available at the time.

So, Adam and Eve covered their nakedness with fig leaves. And it worked. No more shame, no more hiding. And they lived happily ever after...

Umm ... no.

They still hid! This is the earliest recorded result of sin management. It will not work. It hasn't ever worked. When I discover I'm still hiding, that probably should be the hint that whatever I've tried to cover my shame with hasn't taken.

It wasn't until they trusted that God did something—provided His own covering for them—that they could be free from hiding and condemnation. This is still true for me, many centuries later. Any time I hurt another or make wrong choices, the way home is not by attempting to cover my failure through something I can do to pay God off. The way home is not effort, not amends, not heroic promise. The way home is trusting what God paid to cleanse me.

This life in Christ is not about what I can do to make myself worthy of His acceptance, but about daily trusting what He has done to make me worthy of His acceptance.

Back to the garden. On that day, all humanity learned how to look over shoulders; to dart glances; to say one thing and mean another; to hide fear, deceit, and shame behind a nervous smile. That day, we learned how to give the appearance we're someone other than who we actually are.

We begin to lose hope we can be "fixed." So, we cover up. We put on a mask and begin bluffing. After a while, we can barely remember how to live any other way.

SCRIPTURE:

Genesis 3:6-13

REFLECT:

How does it feel to imagine that free, joyful time with God? How have you experienced that?

What formula do you subconsciously believe will make you loved and accepted? We're not talking about what you know you "should" believe, but what your heart really believes.

How does seeing Adam and Eve's original sin management attempt shed light on your attempts to "take care of" your sin?

NOTES

Section 3:

You can find the audio file of this section at trueface.org/two-roads-group.

Mask-wearers fall into a variety of groupings. While there will always be endless variations, these three groups identify most of us.

THOSE TRYING TO CONVINCE OTHERS THEY'RE DOING "JUST FINE"

This crowd is convinced neat, hidden, and tidy are better than authentic and known. They believe God wants us to appear orderly and good, whether we are or not. The appearance of appropriateness and rightness is their highest value. Parents in this group applaud children more for pious behavior than for learning to trust God.

We are surrounded by nicely scrubbed folk who smile broadly and shake each other's hand firmly. Our conversations can go something like this:

"Hi, Carmen. How ya' doin'?"

"Well, hello, Enrique. I'm doin' fine. Can't complain. Fine day we're having. Yep, just fine."

"Oh, yes it is, Carmen. Fine as fine can be. How's that husband of yours?"

"Well, Enrique, he's doin' fine, too. Whole family's a big old basket of fine! Now, just so you can

NOTES

pray effectively, Mrs. Sanderson has it on reliable information that several other unnamed families are not doing fine."

"Well, I'm sure they'll be fine, Carmen. What matters is that we're fine . . . just fine."

This mask hides pain. It covers shame with appearance and a forced smile. We're convinced there is no real help for our issues and the best thing we can do is hide our true identities. If we thought it wouldn't ruin everything, we'd yell out, "You have no idea who I am! Nobody does! Not even my spouse! Even surrounded by friends and family, I'm unknown. When I enter a room full of people, I'm rehearsed. I can make small talk. I can even enter into deep intellectual discussions. But the person you see is made up on the run while the real me is frantically operating levers behind a mask."

If we could take off our masks long enough, many of us would say, "I'm tired. Really tired. I'm weary of hurting, weary of dragging myself through the same hoops I've jumped hundreds of times already. I feel betrayed—by my own behavior, by my community of faith. Everyone there seems to be doing fine. I almost believe they are. That hurts most of all. Mostly, I feel betrayed by God Himself."

Then the mask goes back on, the practiced smile returns and "seldom is heard a discouraging word, and the skies are not cloudy all day."

THOSE STILL SEARCHING FOR THE NEXT "NEW" TECHNIQUE

This group believes there's something preventing them from receiving what everyone else seems to have. They know their life isn't fine. They listen to message after message, podcast after podcast, growing more disillusioned that they'll ever get what others have.

"Just give me something I can add to my game plan to fix me without too much pain and change."

But like dieters on their eleventh plan, we're growing increasingly skeptical. We throw baling wire over our issues, and we know it. There must be a new answer. There has to be. The God we trust wouldn't be playing with our heads . . . would He?

This twisted reasoning begins to creep into our thinking:

What's wrong with me? Nothing works. Maybe, after what I've done, I don't deserve answers. Others seem to figure this stuff out while I stay the same. Nothing is getting me to the abundant life I'm supposed to be experiencing.

We adopt formulas, strategies, and disciplines promising to change us, but we remain ultimately the same. We know it, and we fear others are beginning to

NOTES

NOTES

learn it, too. Maybe we've learned a new vocabulary and can rearrange the furniture on our behaviors, but deep inside, we're pretty sure we're only slightly different than we were. If others could spend a moment inside our heads, they'd be disgusted by what they'd discover. We can't imagine what we'd do if others learned the truth about us. So, we pretend to know more than we do. We offer answers to others, knowing those answers aren't working for us.

We're starting to lose hope that we can change. We suspect that what we're missing is hidden from our ability to fix.

Some reading this are thinking, "Hey, people, get it together! What's wrong with you?" We may soon discover we are part of a third group.

THOSE WEARING THE PEDIGREED MASK

We're the "together" folk, the postcard family: well-educated, well-heeled, well-groomed, well-assured, well-positioned. . . and, well, a lot of work for everyone else.

Our lives don't really have all this messy stuff in it. We can't figure out why there are so many messed-up Christians. "What's the hang-up? Get over it."

We'd never say it, but it feels like we're superior to some extent. We don't really need the help from God others do. We're deeply grateful for what He did on the cross but can't relate to words like "dependence," "needs," "vulnerability," and "unresolved issues." It's just not that hard for us. Our home and family and hobbies are almost as together as we are. Our lawns are immaculate. We don't need help or answers; we are help and answers. At least in our circles, we're the standard others are measuring themselves against. We don't need vulnerability. Vulnerability is for the needy. And needy doesn't keep your lawn immaculate.

We intimidate others. Honestly, we probably should. Most of them are jealous. If they had our self-determination and discipline, they wouldn't have to be intimidated. Their issue ultimately is not with us, but with not being able to live up to their own standard.

. . .

This group is the most maddening to the rest of us. They almost seem like they don't need God in their daily life. They are above such need, somehow. Maybe the Gnostics were right after all. Maybe there really is a superior race of people who don't need God like the rest of us. "Self-managed maturity" is the best way to describe their lives. They don't pretend it's the superiority of their relationship with God that makes them so. There's just something innate that makes them great, and it's almost as if God should be thankful they're here.

They are deeply self-aware and comfortable in their own skin. They display maturity and self-control that those of us who depend on Jesus with our entire beings can't seem to harness. Because of their great

NOTES

67

confidence in their own ability and success, they have little motivation to place their trust in the grace or love of God. They've apparently learned how to live daily life without God. God is a peripheral element to their lives, like a hobby. Their faith makes them that much more well-rounded and healthy. They are aloof to a tender connection with Jesus and sense little need for Him except as the basis for their values and principles. Their only real concern is that something might keep them from becoming the self-actualized "perfect" version of themselves.

This pedigreed group has probably put this book down already. Or they're reading it to better understand their messed-up Uncle Floyd. Ironically, this group may be the neediest, most desperate of all.

Their masks are the hardest to remove because they have the most difficulty admitting their masks are there at all.

While this group's résumé and gentility are impressive, they're still man-made. The pride that put Christ on a cross dwells richly in this group. Their masks, though minimal and elegant, are the most dangerous form of mask. Even grotesque, disfiguring masks at least allow the wearer no doubt he's wearing one.

Here's another problem: Others can't relate. They don't know how to love those with pedigreed masks, how to receive love from them, how to trust. The pedigreed are admired and inspire imitation but

NOTES

are also veiled and unknowable. They are majestic, benevolent emperors—wearing no clothes at all.

SCRIPTURE:

1 John 1:7

REFLECT:

There are many more masks than just these three groups, but of the three, which do you most relate to?

For the mask you most relate to, fill in this sentence for what fits you personally. "If I just _____ then I will _____ ."

We wear masks because we don't want others to see what our true faces look like. What are three words you would use to describe your true self? How did you come up with your words?

NOTES

Section 4:

You can find
the audio file of
this section at
trueface.org/two-
roads-group.

With the exception of the Pedigree Mask group, most of us will, if challenged, admit to wearing masks. We don't like our masks, necessarily, but we have no idea how to take them off. If the thought didn't scare us so much, we'd have shed them long ago, but most of us have no idea where they came from.

That's why revealing the origins of our masks is so important. We need to see ourselves objectively within our story, to see what drives the responses tripping us up. Our controlling behavior is rarely random. It's triggered by unresolved junk, and if we begin to understand the process of unresolved sin, we may no longer react to each new provocation like lemmings sprinting for the nearest cliff. Our masks are a symptom, not a root cause, a fever indicating a raging infection deep inside. We must expose this dark dynamic compelling us to protect ourselves.

OUR REAL PROBLEM:

When we sin, or when someone else sins against us, we automatically respond. If we commit the sin, our automatic response is called guilt. If someone sins against us, our automatic response is called hurt. God graciously designed these two responses to signal that something wrong has happened, that our hearts are disrupted and need healing. We don't work at producing these two responses to sin. They're as

NOTES

natural as the sting we feel when we leave our hand over a flame too long.

Most of us don't know what to do with these internal responses though. Like Adam, we feel naked, so we hide or override our guilt and hurt. In the moment, it seems like necessary self-preservation. But remaining in that choice soon unleashes new depths of pain, inner turmoil, and new masks to wear.

As with an undiagnosed infection spreading poison through our system, we may recognize something is not right. We don't have the energy we used to, and we wince and feel things we hadn't before. Still, we may not connect the dots. An invisible, inner enemy is draining our joy. We may ignore it or stuff it away, and it may lie dormant for a while, but unresolved sin is still there. Bacterial infections often keep spreading poison until antibiotics are introduced. You can dress nicer and comb your hair all you want, but you'll only be a well-dressed sick person with nicely combed hair. No external appearance or vigorous exercise will solve our infection. That is why we named this book *The Cure*.

Nothing in us is equipped or designed to absorb sin.

Even when I'm the one being sinned against, I cannot handle it, because it will always ignite the nature of the sin already in me. So, I give myself permission to respond sinfully. How twisted is that? It makes me want to cry out, "It's not fair! I didn't start this. I wasn't the one who sinned!" It is not fair, but sin doesn't play by the rules.

The transformational good news is that the damage can stop at any time by trusting and applying God's power to resolve that sin. If we don't access God's resources, the devastating pattern continues, and our guilt or hurt will then breed half a dozen uglier responses. We call these inevitable effects: blame, fear, denial, anger, and their assorted sickly relatives. Something under our own roof begins to destroy us, and most of us are clueless about this chain reaction. We only know we have deep painful feelings, distorted, dysfunctional thoughts, and befuddling behaviors we feel the need to mask.

Among the damaging behaviors resulting from unresolved sin:

- We become highly sensitized to our own sin and judge the sin of others.

- We lose our objectivity in a crisis and become the issue.

- We hide our sinful behaviors and become vulnerable to more sin.

- We are unable to love or be loved.

- We become more susceptible to wrong life choices.

- We attempt to control others.

SCRIPTURE:

Psalm 51:3-14

REFLECT:

When you are sinned against and experience hurt, what is your go-to response or inevitable effect? These might be blame, fear, denial, anger, or others.

When you sin against someone and experience guilt, what is your go-to response?

NOTES

Unresolved sin can either be sin done against us or sin we have done against someone else that we haven't processed with God. Is there a situation or relationship of "unresolved sin" that comes to mind in your own personal life? How might that situation have affected other areas of your life?

You can find the audio file of this section at trueface.org/two-roads-group.

NOTES

Section 5:

When we don't resolve our sin—either because we don't know how or choose not to—we release an inevitable force draining our confidence in who we really are.

The next thing we know, we're looking for a top-of-the-line mask, maybe several: "I'm better than most"; "I don't care"; "I'm self-sufficient"; "I'm important"; "I'm competent enough to be loved"; "I have answers others don't"; or "I'm independent." But all the while, our lies whisper, "You're an imposter. You always have been. You always will be. You may fool others, but I know who you are. You're an embarrassment. You have no credibility or self-respect. You spent it long ago."

It's expensive to wear a mask. First, no one—not even those I love—gets to see my face. There are moments when a hint of the real me bleeds through, but mostly I'm as confusing to others as I am to myself. Worse, I never experience the love of others because it's not the real me. So, I sense I'm still not loved and I self-diagnose. Maybe my mask wasn't tight enough, so then I continue searching for a better mask, convinced the next one will give me what I need, prove I'm worthy to receive love. I can't love behind a mask, at least not fully. Those I long to love experience only the cloying attempts of someone who doesn't really exist.

Many of us stopped on those last sentences and sighed at the realization we've wasted years of missed love and stunted maturity.

When we influence wearing a mask, we
convince others:

- They too must live a two-faced life.

- They too must present an idealized person.

- They too must hide what is true about them.

- New life in Christ doesn't really work.

- They will remain stuck in their unresolved
  life issues.

- It is better to be unknown than to risk rejection.

- Self-protection is their only hope.

In the end, we're not just actors. We're also irrational
directors of a badly over-stylized play, teaching those
we love how to pose and masquerade, memorize fake
lines, rehearse expressions, and produce false tears
on command.

Our masks deceive us into believing we can hide our
true selves. We can't. In time, others can usually see
what we're trying to hide. No matter how beautifully
formed, our masks eventually reveal us as warped
figures. All masks eventually crack, buckle, or unravel.

So, why do believers wear more masks than others?
All masks are the product of pretending something in
our lives is true, even if experience denies it. We may
even be fueled by a sincere desire to make God look
good by having our act together. He has no need for
such help, but we think it's our duty. So, we hide our

NOTES

scars and pretend we're modeling to the world how well God treats His followers. Instead, we just come off weird and smug.

The greatest hope for any mask-wearer is in understanding all masks eventually crack and dissolve, gradually revealing what is hidden beneath. All masks crumble because they are man-made.

This is a good thing, though. Imagine if the mask didn't crack. It would forever separate us from love, authenticity, and freedom. We could go our entire lives missing what we were created to enjoy. Our endlessly loving God allows our masks to fall apart because He cares so deeply for us.

Once we weary enough of mask-wearing, we can begin rediscovering the true face of Jesus. He is the centerpiece in the Room of Grace. Jesus will always nudge us further out into the open, allowing our true faces to be revealed. Our true faces are beautiful, too. God made them exactly the way He wanted, and He longs to see His reflection. The trouble with papier-mâché is, it doesn't reflect.

All of us wake up one day to the pain of realizing we can't control our lives the way we thought we could. We're still stuck with unresolved issues, symptoms we're trying to fix, without anyone's help.

Only that sort of revelation will free me into the stunning, life-giving hope of this next statement:

"What if there was a place so safe that the worst of me could be known, and I would discover that I would not be loved less but more in the telling of it?"

That place exists. And when you reach it, unresolved issues will begin to heal. You'll gather up stacks of masks and toss them in the dumpster, brushing your hands together as you walk away. Then, you'll walk out into the daylight, your skin feeling the morning air for the first time since you can remember. You'll drink in the beauty of flowers and earth, free from those nauseating fumes of epoxy holding your face to a mask.

SCRIPTURE:

2 Corinthians 3:18

REFLECT:

Who do you influence? Everyone has influence whether they intend to or not. You might have influence with your coworkers, your friends, your kids, your spouse, your boss, your employees, and many others. What are you teaching them about masks, both through your words and—perhaps more importantly—through your behavior?

How do you grow in believing that your true face, the one that God made just how He wanted it, is beautiful? How does it feel to try to believe that?

Let yourself sit for a moment with this statement. "What if there was a place so safe that the worst of me could be known, and I would discover that I would not be loved less but more in the telling of it?" Can you imagine that kind of place? What does it feel like? When have you experienced that in a relationship or community?

Week 3

Who am I?

MEETING TOGETHER

This week we're going to study what scripture says about who we are, who God is, and why that means we can live in authentic community.

Connect

🕐 **30% OF YOUR TIME**

- Pray to open this time together. Who wants to volunteer?

- Warm-up question:

  » If practicality or income wasn't an issue, what would be your dream job?

- Check in questions:

  » Last week we talked about practical, tangible ways we can start taking off our masks. How did that play out this past week? If you didn't take the step you chose last week, what do you think held you back?

  » What stood out to you this week, either from our conversation last time or the Digging Deeper material? What questions came up?

Learn

 20% OF YOUR TIME

First, have someone read John 17:20-26 out loud for the group (the NLT version is below).

> **THEN, WATCH THE STUDY VIDEO.**
> You'll find this at *trueface.org/two-roads-group.*

SCRIPTURE:

John 17:20-26 NLT

20 "I am praying not only for these disciples but also for all who will ever believe in me through their message. 21 I pray that they will all be one, just as you and I are one—as you are in me, Father, and I am in you. And may they be in us so that the world will believe you sent me.

22 "I have given them the glory you gave me, so they may be one as we are one. 23 I am in them and you are in me. May they experience such perfect unity that the world will know that you sent me and that you love them as much as you love me. 24 Father, I want these whom you have given me to be with me where I am. Then they can see all the glory you gave me because you loved me even before the world began!

25 "O righteous Father, the world doesn't know you, but I do; and these disciples know you sent me. 26 I have revealed you to them, and I will continue to do so. Then your love for me will be in them, and I will be in them."

Live

 50% OF YOUR TIME

TIME OF REFLECTION:

Have someone else read John 17:20-26 again. Then set aside five to ten minutes to reflect on this passage with the Lord in silence. Use the prayer and questions below as a guide.

> *Tip: As you re-read this passage a few times, allow yourself to pause on certain statements, underline what stands out, or take notes.*

Jesus, help me to understand your Living Word. Help me to hear the truth of who you are, how you love me, and how you see me as your beloved child and holy saint. Help me to hear your Spirit speak to me about what this passage means for me today. Thank you for making this possible.

- What verse stands out to me?

- What do I believe with my head and not my heart in these passages?

- God, what do you want to communicate to me through this?

NOTES

DISCUSS:

After your reflection time, choose a few questions
that jump out to you from the list below to process as
a group. Do your best to not give the answer you think
you're supposed to—try to be as authentic and real
as you can.

1. What did you feel like God was wanting to
   communicate to you through that passage?

2. What stood out to you in the video?

3. If the Spirit of God now lives in us, then we must
   be holy. God cannot abide in unholiness. How
   does that change how we see ourselves?

4. How would your life be different if you believed
   to the depths of your heart that God the
   Father loves you as much as He loves Jesus?
   Be specific—make it personal. What would
   change for *you*?

5. Jesus begins by saying that He is praying for us
   so that we may *all be one*. How would seeing
   ourselves as unified, holy saints change how we
   live in community?

APPLY:

Move your group discussion into how we can grow in
these areas with the following questions.

- What would it look like for you to believe you are a
  fully accepted saint in your everyday life?

NOTES

NOTES

- In this next week, the Digging Deeper material is going to look at our identity. What is one practical, tangible way that you can step more deeply into your identity this week? Ideas to get you started:

  » Read Galatians 5:22-25 each morning and remind yourself that these descriptors are true of your new heart.

  » Set an alarm on your phone to go off at the same time every day that has a reminder of one aspect of your identity that is hard for you to believe.

  » Write out a shame message you often repeat to yourself (e.g. "I'm so stupid," "I'm a bad friend," "I'm too much for people"). Then write out what Jesus says is true about you.

  » Schedule time with someone you trust to share with them a part of John 17:20-26 that you struggle to believe is true for *you*.

  » Anything else come to mind? Be creative, but practical. Try to make it an actionable step in order to help integrate your actions with your beliefs.

- How I'm going to live it out:

- How can the group come alongside you in this?

 Group Tip: Whenever someone in the group shares something significant about what they learned and how they hope to apply it in their lives, make a plan to follow up with them. Put a mark on your calendar 1, 2, or 6 months from now with a note to check in with this person. It is a way to love them well, as well as process ways that the change they hoped for faced speedbumps, impacted their life, or is still in process.

- Pray to close out this time together.

NOTES

03

Digging Deeper

If you're a visual learner, over the next seven days (or however long you're taking between meeting together) read these five sections and reflect on the questions at the end. If you're an auditory learner and would prefer to listen to the sections, we've provided the audio for each day at *trueface.org/two-roads-group.*

You can do them all at once, but we suggest breaking the five sections over multiple days to give you more processing time. This week's sections are from Chapter 3 of *The Cure.*

If you aren't able to go through the five sections before your next meeting, that's okay. Don't let it stop you from connecting with your community.

Section 1:

You can find the audio file of this section at trueface.org/two-roads-group.

NOTES

I left the Room of Grace last week. I didn't tell anyone. I just walked out.

I failed again. As much as I wanted to, when I needed it most I couldn't handle Jesus's arm around me. The whole thing sounds so great until I screw up.

So, late one night, I slipped out and found my way back to the Room of Good Intentions. It's a long walk from the fork to either destination, but there's a direct path between the Room of Grace and the Room of Good Intentions, so it actually isn't far at all. The path skirts the coastline, and it's gorgeous by night, but I didn't pay much attention. Soon the path wound back into the woods, and the Room of Good Intentions loomed ahead over the trees. Soon enough, I broke into a clearing and there it was, the gleaming marble towering above me. The familiarity of it all immediately enveloped me, like an old hooded sweatshirt. I stood there, hands in pockets, for maybe an hour, staring at my sin. Though the heat off the mound of my garbage obscured me from seeing Jesus, I imagined Him on the other side, shaking His head in disappointment. Disrupting His holiness with my selfishness felt . . . it's strange, I know, but it felt right. It felt like what I deserved.

I was jolted out of the moment by a voice behind me on the path. "You know, if you really want to sneak out, you're gonna need to shut the door more quietly."

I turned as the voice emerged from the shadows, and
I was startled by his face. It was the loud guy with the
chronic lower-back pain.

"You done here yet?"

"What do you mean?"

"I mean, let's get out of here. I'm not dressed for this
crowd. I'm in my pajamas."

I could see that he was. "How did you know to
find me here?"

"Where else would you go? I used to make the
pilgrimage myself often enough."

"Really? I'm not the only who's done this?"

"Oh, it happens all the time. Soon as you walked out
the door, someone yelled, 'We got a runner!' I figured
it might be you. So, I started walking. Look, you don't
have to come back with me. Stay as long as you
like. I just wanted to make sure you weren't beating
yourself up."

"I was."

"I know."

Without a word, he turned and I followed.

NOTES

After a while, back on the path winding toward the coast, I asked, "Why did I do that? Why did I come back here? That first day in the Room of Grace I thought I'd never see life the same."

"You don't see life the same. But the stories we tell ourselves can run deep. It's one thing to have a profound experience, and it's quite another to kill a lie that's served you a long time. Especially a lie you've used to cope. Until you see God right, you'll keep going back there."

"What's that supposed to mean?"

"There are two gods: the one we see through our shame, and the One who actually is."

"Okay . . . I think I'm tracking here."

"So, think back to what you told me about Jesus with His arm around you. Did you believe it?"

"Yeah, I guess I'm starting to. But . . ." I trailed off.

"But what?" he asked.

"Well, when I pictured it later, His arm is around me, but He's not smiling. He's got this look of pity. There's no joy. It's like a friend comforting a dying patient, someone who's sick and never gets any better. And there's never anyone else around. He's disappointed in me. But He loves me enough to keep holding on. I

know He won't leave me . . . I just didn't turn out like
He hoped."

"Ah. My friend, you're still believing in the god your
shame created, the god you've learned to fear."

"This is all so hard to wrap my head around," I said.
"Everything I've ever been taught—everything I've
ever experienced—tells me you get what you put in.
So, when I fail, it seems only right I should get less
of God, which makes me want to be better. I want to
put in more, so I'll get out more. Then I get down on
myself when I take Him for granted or when I don't do
right, or when I care about something more than Him.
That seems like what He wants. If I were God, that's
what I'd want out of people."

He laughed. "That seems pretty self-righteous,
doesn't it?"

"You're saying it's not?"

"Let me say it again: You have as much God as you're
gonna get! He lives in you! You are in Him. How much
closer do you want than that? Every moment of every
day, fused with you, there He is. He never moves,
never covers His ears when you sin, never puts up a
newspaper, never turns His back. He's not over on
the other side of your sin, waiting for you to get it
together so you can finally be close. It's incredible!
Don't you think? That's why they call it 'Good News'!"

"Then why doesn't it feel like it?" I blurted, then sighed to level myself. "I live with me. It feels like I'm playing a game of denial to believe He's not disappointed with me. I know He loves me, but where's the accountability to live this life for Him?"

The woods thinned and cleared, giving way to grassy dunes and eventually the sea. It was all lit up by the moon, nearly clear as day. I couldn't believe I didn't notice it earlier. My new friend looked at it all thoughtfully, like he was trying to find another way of explaining what I was missing. After a moment, he turned back.

"The goal is not to change me. I'm already changed. The goal is to mature.

When I depend on the new creature I've been made into through the work of Jesus at the cross, I begin to live healthier, more free of sin, more free to love. I learn to believe all His power, love, truth, and goodness already exists in me, right now. Even on my worst day."

"But if people believe this, won't they take advantage of God?"

"Yeah, I imagine they would," he responded. "Except they no longer want to do such a thing. They are new creations. God lives in them to encourage, correct, and even rebuke. The reason people rebel is not because they trusted grace or chose to live out their new identity. It's the very opposite. It is moralism, the law of religious practice and thought, that keeps them trying to get away with something."

"Wow. I've never heard anyone say that."

"Look, Jesus says we really are new people, completely righteous. Jesus became sin so we might be righteous. Jesus didn't become theoretical sin. He actually became real sin, in every possible way that sin can be sin. And if the corollary holds, then we didn't become theoretical righteousness. We became real righteousness in every possible way that righteousness can be righteousness. That didn't happen to anyone before Jesus. Now we're free. But it isn't the freedom to get away with stuff, to give ourselves permission to have three glasses of wine instead of one. It isn't freedom to care less or walk the tightrope of right and wrong without remorse. The motive of a righteous heart is not to get away with anything. The motive of the righteous is to be loved and to love! That's what we've all been wanting for all of history. That's the freedom Jesus died for. We can now love each other well because it's who we really are."

Then it was silent for a while, just the waves and the moon and a soft wind. Then, when the horizon faded from blue black into purple and finally into orange as the sun peeked out over the waves, we walked again, together, all the way back to the Room of Grace.

NOTES

SCRIPTURE:

2 Corinthians 5:17

REFLECT:

One "aha" moment doesn't resolve the deep and habitual shame stories we tell ourselves. What does it look like to give yourself grace when you realize you've returned to the Room of Good Intentions or returned to one of your shame stories?

Think back to a time that you learned "you get what you put in" in relationships. How do you think that has that affected your relationship with God?

"The goal is not to change me. I'm already changed. The goal is to mature." Think about one area of your life that you would like to be different—perhaps you'd like to experience more patience or more courage. How does it change the way you approach that when you think, "I want to change into a patient person," versus, "I want to mature into the patient person Jesus says I truly am"?

Section 2:

Your view of you is the greatest commentary on your view of God.

Nothing you believe and depend upon is more magnificently freeing than this single truth:

you are no longer who you were, even on your worst day.

Trusting and leaning upon "Christ in you" is the source of every shred of strength, joy, healing, and peace.

What we believe happened in that first moment of trusting Jesus affects everything. That start is called "justification," which means to be made right. Think about what it means to believe you were made right.

Some believe they will eventually, through sincere diligence, change into someone better. Their confidence to change centers on sanctified self-effort.

Others believe the very essence of who they now are is completely changed. They are convinced of absolute fused union with the God of the universe.

Their confidence to mature is placed squarely in trust of their new identity in Jesus.

You can find the audio file of this section at trueface.org/two-roads-group.

NOTES

This does not mean they don't fail. They do fail. But in the end, they trust who God has made them.

If I follow the first path, I'm trying to change from who I was into who I should be. If I follow the second, I'm maturing into who I already am. In the first, I'm working toward becoming more righteous. In the second, I'm already righteous, made right by God in the moment I believed.

There were seasons early on when I believed:

- I have been changed into a new creature. I am fused with Jesus.
- He loves me and enjoys me all the time.
- He is maturing me in His way, in His time.
- I can trust and receive love.

Most of the rest of my time I've believed:

- I changed in a legal sense, but not really.
- He is usually disappointed with me.
- He expects me to at least try to fix myself.
- I can't be trusted or trust anyone else.

This is the cruel joke we play on ourselves: to bluff and pretend we are righteous, secretly knowing we aren't, only to eventually discover we actually were all along.

Much of our difficulty accepting this new life has to do with the shame we carry. Shame. It whispers and hisses that no matter what you do, you will always be defined by what you did or what was done to you. It mocks you. Shame wants you desperately performing for acceptance you don't believe you deserve.

That's when we begin to form the fake god. We imagine Him staring at us with a thin smile and a measured nod. He has to love us, but He's not sure He likes us. His arms are folded. He wears an expression that says, "Yes, your sins are forgiven. Your ticket's punched for eternity. But don't get lazy! You've got to stop being such a slug. And don't think I missed that last wrong thought you had four minutes ago. I'm not stupid. I still keep a list. I just don't lose my temper as much. What are you staring at? Get to work!"

How can we draw close to a god we imagine saying, "Sure, your sins are forgiven, but you're still the same failure. You had an excuse before, but not anymore."

SCRIPTURE:

Colossians 2:9-10

REFLECT:

When you mess up, what expression do you picture on God's face?

How would believing that you're no longer who you were, even on your worst day, change how you respond to messing up or failing?

NOTES

Which of the "Most of the rest of the time, I've believed" statements most stands out to you? How does believing that affect your other close relationships?

Section 3:

What difference does any of this make in what you and I are facing right now?

Let's consider one area many struggle with: sexual sin.

Almost every book on fighting sexual sin focuses on how we can react better at the moment of temptation. Hundreds of tips and techniques are laid out to keep us from acting out. While helpful, these books miss the point: we didn't reach this moment randomly.

We got here by gradually distorting our view of God back there.

Those prevention tools made sense until we allowed ourselves to entertain a thought that would eventually lead us into crisis. The moment those safeguards are needed, it's too late. We no longer want them to help. We are now way past wanting to do right. The problem is actually rooted far back when our course was fundamentally altered. The problem is our distorted picture of God.

That distortion is a pall over our eyes, keeping light out.

You can find the audio file of this section at trueface.org/two-roads-group.

NOTES

That distortion is there because we believe these five things about God:

1. God can't satisfy me as much as this sin.

2. I've always been this way. I don't believe I'm powerful enough to change that.

3. There is something fundamentally wrong with me.

4. I don't believe God has been fully good to me.

5. I'm going to feel like a failure anyway, so I might as well enjoy it!

These are the root beliefs behind the permission we give ourselves to fail. They all are formed from picturing God separated from us.

At that point, it's only a matter of time, opportunity, and our particular areas of vulnerability.

That's why this is a big deal.

Those in the Room of Grace are continually allowing God to work on removing the pall from their eyes. Light pours in, and they are in the process of being freed to live beyond preoccupation over their next failure.

Those in the Room of Good Intentions are rarely willing to confront those five statements. They're too busy covering their tracks and grinding it out against temptation. The great regret is that they know they've already given themselves permission to fail.

In fact, the insidious truth about sin is that fighting it only serves to heighten the anticipated pleasure.

If you ever want to truly connect with a family member or friend who has issues of repeated failure, reaching the root of those five distortions about God will help you resolve and heal sin issues exponentially better than techniques tailored to a moment, or prevention gimmicks that work just fine until you don't want them to. The fruit will be a lifetime of conversation, hope, protection, and healing.

If we see God through a veil of shame, we'll think the goal is to "fix" the behavior. Shame wants us constantly trying to prove we're not as bad as we imagine. In the Room of Grace, however, we're learning to believe we are no longer identified by shame. Our God doesn't see us that way, and He doesn't need us to see ourselves that way. We're free to trust His delight and love even in the midst of our erratic, maturing behaviors. He wants us to learn dependence on Him instead of performance. We're learning to trust His power in us. The beauty is, we actually fail less in doing so.

NOTES

SCRIPTURE:

Romans 8:1

REFLECT:

Which of the five distortions do you most connect with? In your particular patterns of sin, where does this distortion fit?

Striving to sin less does not mean we will love more. How have you experienced this?

Try to imagine yourself in a situation where you're being tempted to sin. Now imagine God looking at you, with full delight and love, inviting you to trust that He has better things ahead. How is this different than how you normally feel when you're in this kind of situation?

Section 4:

Okay. So how do we know whether our relationship is with the god we see through our shame or the God who really is?

You can find the audio file of this section at **trueface.org/two-roads-group**.

Well, probably I'd have to ask what shame looks like in a relationship:

- Do I measure my closeness to God by how little I'm sinning or by my trust that, to the exact extent the Father loves Jesus, Jesus loves me?

- Do I see myself primarily as a "saved sinner" or a "saint who still sins"?

- When I talk to God, do I spend more time rehearsing my failures or enjoying His presence?

- Am I drawn to severe authors and preachers who challenge me to "get serious about sin" or those who encourage me to trust this new identity in me?

- Is my hard effort being spent preoccupied with sin or in expressing and receiving love from others?

- Do I trust disciplines to make me strong or grace to strengthen me?

- Do I read the Bible as "You ought. You should. Why can't you? When will you?" or as "You can. This is who you now are"?

NOTES

SCRIPTURE:

Colossians 3:12-17

REFLECT:

Circle which of the two you most believe in each statement (we know sometimes we're right between the two). Do you see any patterns to what you circled?

As you look at how you perceive God overall, what is one truth about God that, if you were to really trust it, would be transformative? Spend some time in scripture looking for a verse that articulates this truth.

Read Colossians 3:12-17. First read it with the mindset of, "You ought. You should. Why can't you? When will you?" Then read it as, "You can. This is who you now are." What do you feel in each reading?

NOTES

Section 5:

It may feel like a gamble to you, but it is no gamble to God.

God has shown all of His cards, revealing breathtaking protection. He says, in essence, "What if I tell them who they now are? What if I take away any element of fear? What if I tell them I will always love them? That I love them right now, as much as I love my only Son?

"What if I tell them there are no logs of past offenses, of how little they pray or how often they've let me down? What if I tell them they are actually righteous right now? What if I tell them I'm crazy about them? What if I tell them that, if I'm their Savior, they're going to heaven no matter what—it's a done deal? What if I tell them they have a new nature, that they are saints, not saved sinners? What if I tell them I actually live in them now, my love, power, and nature at their disposal?

"What if I tell them they don't have to put on masks? That they don't need to pretend we're close?

"What if they knew that, when they mess up, I'll never retaliate? What if they were convinced bad circumstances aren't my way of evening the score? What if they knew the basis of our friendship isn't how little they sin, but how much they allow me to love them? What if I tell them they can hurt my heart but

You can find the audio file of this section at trueface.org/two-roads-group.

NOTES

I'll never hurt theirs? What if I tell them they can open their eyes when they pray and still go to heaven? What if I tell them there is no secret agenda, no trapdoor? What if I tell them it isn't about their self-effort, but about allowing me to live my life through them?"

Nature provides many examples of this incredible discrepancy between who we appear to be and who we truly are. Consider the caterpillar. If we brought a caterpillar to a biologist and asked him to analyze it and describe its DNA, he would tell us, "I know this looks like a caterpillar to you. But scientifically, according to every test, including DNA, this is fully and completely a butterfly." Wow! God has wired into a creature looking nothing like a butterfly a perfectly complete butterfly identity. And because the caterpillar is a butterfly in essence, it will one day display the behavior and attributes of a butterfly. The caterpillar matures into what is already true about it. In the meantime, berating the caterpillar for not being more like a butterfly is not only futile, it will probably hurt its tiny ears!

So it is with us. God has given us the DNA of righteousness. We are saints. Nothing we do will make us more righteous than we already are. Nothing we do will alter this reality. God knows our DNA. He knows that we are "Christ in me." And now He is asking us to join Him in what He knows is true!

THE BEST THING YOU COULD DO

It is hard to grasp how incredibly this would free our world, our children, our friends, our church, our neighborhood, our businesses, ourselves—everything—if we choose to believe it!

The best thing you could do at this moment is to put this book down, lace up your shoes, and take a long, slow walk through the neighborhood, and imagine. Imagine such a life.

Once you can imagine it, you can start to consider the risk and reward of it.

Once you can consider it, you can begin to believe it. Once you can believe it, you can begin to risk trying it out. Once you try it out, you can begin to enjoy it.

Once you can enjoy it, you will find others to join you. Once someone joins you, others will follow.

And once others follow . . .

Well, you get where this is going.

So, here we are, daring to risk believing that His arm is around us and He is not embarrassed or disgusted. Maybe I'm beginning to grasp the concept for moments at a time, that I have at this exact moment all of God I'm ever going to get here on earth. And to

enjoy it and avail myself of it, all I have to do is trust!
We feel seditious and frightened to even imagine
thinking such a thing. But there it is. And now the
fun begins.

Well, out into the night air with you. We'll be here
when you get back.

SCRIPTURE:

John 3:16-18

REFLECT:

*The best thing you could do, right now, is let yourself
really think about such a life. So, go. We'll leave you some
space to write down your thoughts when you're ready,
but we think it's time for you to go talk with your Father
about this amazing life He's inviting you to.*

Week 4

How could this change my life?

MEETING TOGETHER

This week, we're going to look at how we can go and live in this new reality of God's love and our identity, and how that can transform our relationships.

Connect

 40% OF YOUR TIME

As a group:

- Pray to begin this time together. Who wants to volunteer?

- Warm-up question:

  » What has been an area of your life that you have trusted God or someone else with over the past month?

- Take ten minutes to do the self-assessment on the next page individually.

WHERE AM I NOW?

On a scale of 1–5, how much do you agree or disagree with the following statements?

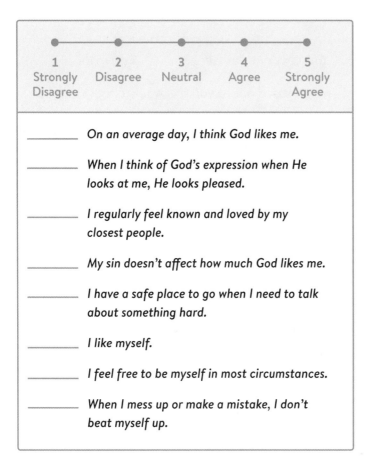

1	2	3	4	5
Strongly Disagree	Disagree	Neutral	Agree	Strongly Agree

_____ On an average day, I think God likes me.

_____ When I think of God's expression when He looks at me, He looks pleased.

_____ I regularly feel known and loved by my closest people.

_____ My sin doesn't affect how much God likes me.

_____ I have a safe place to go when I need to talk about something hard.

_____ I like myself.

_____ I feel free to be myself in most circumstances.

_____ When I mess up or make a mistake, I don't beat myself up.

Now, go back and look at the assessment at the beginning of this study on page 9. Spend some time reflecting on what is different about the way you view God and yourself.

NOTES

Come back together as a group, and talk through these questions:

- What is one thing you notice from when you first took the assessment to now?

- Last week we talked about practical, tangible ways we can start walking in our true identity. How did that play out this week?

- What stood out to you this week, either from our conversation last time or the Digging Deeper material? What questions came up?

Learn

 10% OF YOUR TIME

> ▶ **WATCH THE LIVE VIDEO.**
> You'll find this at *trueface.org/two-roads-group.*

Live

 50% OF YOUR TIME

DISCUSS:

Choose a few questions that jump out at you from the list below to process as a group.

1 What stood out to you in the video?

2 What emotions come up when you imagine a life of authentic community and relationships?

3 What is the biggest barrier that would prevent you from living in a Room of Grace?

4 What is one area in which this group can grow as a Room of Grace?

5 What has been a standout moment or takeaway from this four session experience?

APPLY:

- In this next week, what is one practical, tangible way that you can go and live out this good news of freedom, joy, and authenticity? Here are some ideas to get you started:

  » Make a list of things that make you—the real you—feel joy. Pick one of those and go do it this week, believing that God thinks you're worth taking care of.

  » Plan a small dinner party of friends and choose one probing question for the group to discuss.

  » Try out our "Affirmation in Your Family" tool at trueface.org/books.

  » Write out some truths from this study and tape them up places you'll remember them (e.g. "God likes me," "I'm not who I was, even on my worst day," or "God has His arm around me").

NOTES

» Go through "Beyond the Mask: A Trueface Relational Journey" with someone that you want to go deeper with and invite into this life at trueface.org/journey.

» Anything else come to mind? Be creative, but practical. Try to make it an actionable step in order to help integrate your actions with your beliefs.

- How I'm going to live it out:

- How can the group come alongside you in this?

 Group Tip: Remember to celebrate together. We often don't take time to celebrate growth, life change, or milestones in the maturing process. Being able to celebrate together can help build connection and gratitude for what God has done in our lives.

- We've been looking at applications week to week so far. Let's look a little farther ahead. What would you like to be different in your life in six months based on what you've been learning with this group?

- Pray to close out this time together.

04

Digging Deeper

Go and live. Shake off the shame, the fake smiles, or the shallow conversation. Dig in and prioritize relationships.

Remember, Jesus has already transformed you into a new creation, fully loved, and fully accepted. He is offering you a beautiful, adventurous life of freedom. He's inviting you into authentic, abiding relationships where you are known and loved. So, go and live!

If you're looking for more resources, head to *Trueface.org.*

We have additional books, studies, and experiences to help you continue building high trust communities of grace and inviting others to come and experience this life alongside you. You can also connect with thousands of others living the Trueface life on social media:

Instagram: @truefacelife

Facebook: @truefacecommunity

Twitter: @truefaced

NOTES